Choosing to be
BETTER
Not
BITTER

Written and illustrated by
Carmen Garner

To the Reader,

What we share in common makes us human. How we differ makes us individuals. A household can be made up of two parents, one parent, or no parents. When life gets rough, talk to someone. If your parents are unavailable you can speak with a friend, teacher, coach or possibly a mentor to discuss any personal issues you may encounter.

Thank you Lord for blessing me with the ability to help heal our youth. Thank you for blessing me with a beautiful wife Sabrina, daughter Aarin, and son Carmen Jr.

Lord, thank you, for placing people on my path, a path that leads to a place where our youth are products of Decision Making and Not Circumstance.

Special thank you to Dan Graham. As a Production Artist, he recognized my efforts to reach young people in a creative way, which is why he volunteered his services. Dan's contributions brought depth and life to this project. The youth and I will forever be indebted.

One day a young boy named Ben lost his dog.
It hurt the boy so much.

Ben chose to talk to his parents about his feelings.
In a few days the boy began to feel better!

One day a young boy named Bill lost his dog.
It hurt the boy so much.

Bill chose NOT to talk to his parents and kept
his feelings to himself. In a few days, Bill began to feel bitter.
Feeling bitter can sometimes make you break things.

One day Ben's dad had to go far away for work.
Ben was confused and hurt.

Ben chose to talk to his parents. They told him that although
they would not see each other for a while they would
be together soon. Ben began to feel better!

One day Bill found out his dad was leaving for the Army.
Bill was confused and hurt.

Bill chose NOT to talk to his parents about his feelings. He did
not accept the change. Bill blamed himself and began to feel
bitter. Feeling bitter can sometimes make you say mean things.

One day Ben's turtle died.
Ben was very hurt, angry, and sad.

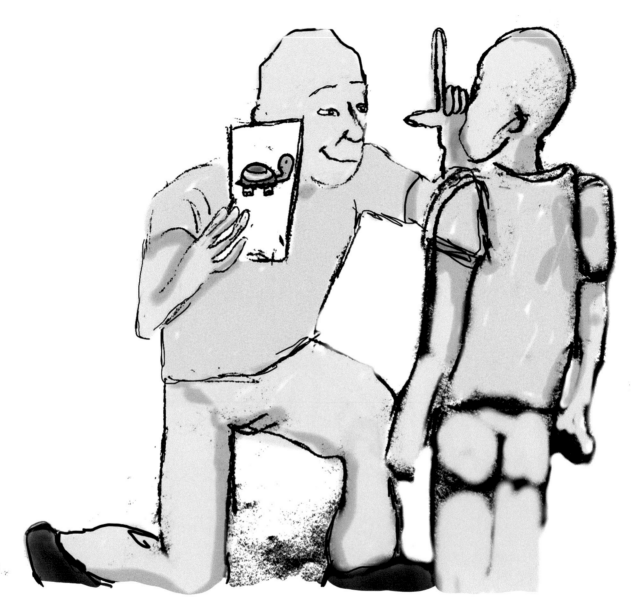

Even though Ben was hurt, angry, and sad, he chose to talk to his parents. Ben learned that his turtle was safe in heaven. This made Ben feel better!

One day Bill's turtle died.
Bill was very hurt, angry, and sad.

Even though Bill was very hurt, angry, and sad, he chose NOT to talk about his turtle and kept his feelings to himself. Soon Bill began to feel bitter. Feeling bitter can sometimes make you feel lonely.

One day Ben's uncle went to jail.

Ben was very hurt and disappointed.

He was Ben's favorite uncle!

Ben was confused. He could not understand why his uncle had to go to jail. His uncle was a good person. Ben chose to talk to his parents. Ben's parents explained to him that people sometimes make mistakes— even good people—and one day he would see his uncle again.
This made Ben feel much better!

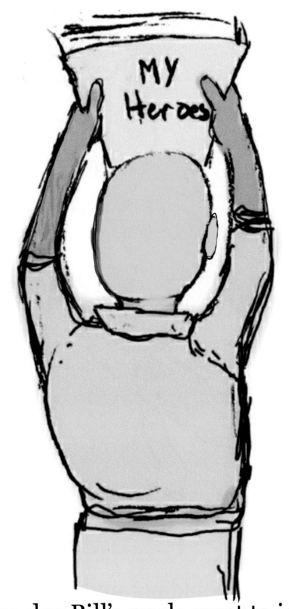

One day Bill's uncle went to jail.
Bill was very hurt and disappointed.
He was Bill's favorite uncle!

Bill was confused. He could not understand why the police arrested his uncle. Bill chose NOT to talk about his feelings. He became very angry. Soon Bill became bitter. Feeling bitter can sometimes make you disrespect authority.

One day Ben was playing with his ball and accidentally
broke his bedroom window. Ben was scared because
he did not know if his parents would be upset.

Ben chose to tell the truth. The boy told his parents that he
broke the window while playing ball in the house. His parents
were pleased that he told the truth. Ben's parents told
him that accidents happen. This made Ben feel better!

One day Bill was playing with his ball and accidentally broke
a window in the house. Bill was scared because he did
not know if his parents would be upset.

Bill chose NOT to tell the truth. He told his parents that he
did not break the window. His parents were not pleased with
him because he told a lie. Bill had to pay for the window with
his allowance money and became even more bitter.
Feeling bitter can make you hide the truth.

One day Ben's father lost his job. Ben's family would have
to move far away to Garnerville. Ben would have to change
schools. Also, Ben would have to make new friends.

At the new school Ben saw Bill, who appeared to be very bitter. Bill seemed angry and hurt. Ben felt sorry for Bill and attempted to introduce himself. Before Ben knew what happened...

Ben continued to be bullied by bitter Bill. The thoughtful boy, Ben, chose to tell his parents. Ben's parents told him to try and talk to the bitter boy to see if they had anything in common.

Ben talked to bitter Bill.

They found out that they had a lot in common!

Both of their dogs ran away, both of their turtles passed,

both of their uncles went to jail, they both broke windows,

and both of their fathers had to leave for a long time.

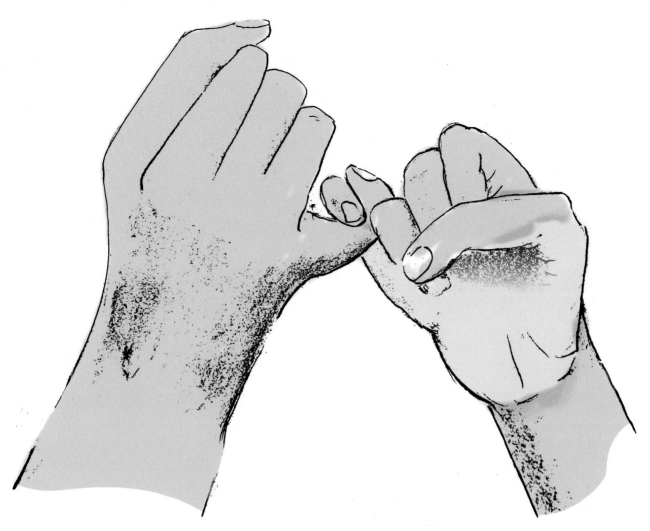

One day a bitter boy met a thoughtful boy who made good decisions about his feelings. The bitter boy listened to and talked with the thoughtful boy. The bitter boy began to feel better. Ben and Bill are now good friends and they both make better decisions!

Print information available on the last page

Rev. date: 05/18/2018

To order additional copies of this book, contact:
Xlibris
1-888-795-4274
www.Xlibris.com
Orders@Xlibris.com

Printed in the United States
By Bookmasters